Young Writers' 16th Annual Poetry Competition

It is feeling and force of imagination that make us eloquent.

How can I not dream while writing? The blank page gives a right to dream.

Verses From
The Heart Of England
Edited by Claire Tupholme

 Young**Writers**

First published in Great Britain in 2007 by:
Young Writers
Remus House
Coltsfoot Drive
Peterborough
PE2 9JX
Telephone: 01733 890066
Website: www.youngwriters.co.uk

SB ISBN 978-1 84602 875 5

Foreword

This year, the Young Writers' *Away With Words* competition proudly presents a showcase of the best poetic talent selected from thousands of up-and-coming writers nationwide.

Young Writers was established in 1991 to promote the reading and writing of poetry within schools and to the young of today. Our books nurture and inspire confidence in the ability of young writers and provide a snapshot of poems written in schools and at home by budding poets of the future.

The thought, effort, imagination and hard work put into each poem impressed us all and the task of selecting poems was a difficult but nevertheless enjoyable experience.

We hope you are as pleased as we are with the final selection and that you and your family continue to be entertained with *Away With Words Verses From The Heart Of England* for many years to come.

Contents

Zoe Bright (12)	81
Ellie Smith (12)	82
Sophie Clay (12)	83
Rebecca Johnson (12)	84
Sam Newbold (12)	85
Charlotte Deall (12)	86
Shaun Gibbs (11)	87
Kezia Purslow (11)	88
Katherine Key (12)	89
Sam Booth (12)	90
Molly Stowe (12)	91
Isaac Alcock (12)	92

Sir Thomas Boughey High School, Stoke-on-Trent
Jessica Cope (16)	93
Naomi Marfleet Lakin (11)	94

Thomas Telford School, Telford
Thomas Turley (11)	95
Phoebe Calloway (12)	96
Jennifer West (11)	97
Jake Swan (11)	98
Edie Harris (12)	99
Daniella Nicholls (12)	100
Emily Crewe (11), Lauren Pestana, Lauren Ramkin & Rebecca Flynn	101
Catherine Hutchinson (11)	102
Rebekah Jeffries (11)	103
Nicole Carr (12)	104
Daisy Clifford (11)	105
Shannon Finnigan (12)	106
Lauren Jones (11)	107
Joshua Bowdley (12)	108
Thomas Knowles (11)	109
Robyn Whitehouse (11)	110
Peter Swift (11)	111
Kieran Baker (11)	112
Simon Harrison (11)	113
Connor Graham (11)	114
Jaskiran Deol (12)	115
Josh Morby (11)	116

Two Rivers 6th Form, Tamworth

The Poems

Why I Love You!

Your smile always seems to brighten my day,
While your words just blow me away.
You're always there by my side,
When I'm upset your arms are open wide.
Your love sets me free,
So people can see the real me.
I only wish that some day you will hold me tight,
You're always stuck in my head from morning to night.
If only you knew how I feel,
Then you'd know my love for you is real.

Charlotte Mottram (12)
King Edward VI High School, Stafford

Away With Words

I have a dog called Simba
She's gold and she's very fast
She used to fight like a ninja
But she's not so aggressive now at last.

My dog's cute and greedy
She eats lots of fruit
Her eyes are ever so beady
She even chews my wellie boot.

My dog likes to play with other doggies
She likes to have a good run
She especially likes to chase the moggies
Her favourite food is a little chocolate bun.

Jamie Corson (12)
King Edward VI High School, Stafford

Polar Bear

A polar bear's fur is like sugar,
his nose is like a black plum,
he lurks around the Arctic
the ground all covered in snow.

A polar bear blends to the background,
he fishes with his big claws,
he may look cute on the outside,
but inside he's like Jaws.

He scratches, he claws into the snow,
he hunts, he kills, it's what he does best,
he plays in the snow wherever he goes
and at night all he does is sleep.

Megan Macpherson (12)
King Edward VI High School, Stafford

Homeless

I have no home,
I am all alone,
My dad had to go away,
My mum left me two years ago this May.
All I have to eat is mouldy bread,
That I found by a doll's head.

I wear a dress
That I found by a pile of mess.
I sleep on a pile of rags,
And a couple of plastic bags.

Every night I wish for someone to come,
Guess who? My mum.
I lie awake wondering if she's still alive,
I wonder if she still loves me, like she did when I was five.

I daren't go far where people can see me,
Because they will put me in care like me friend Lee.
He was a good friend
Until the end.

That was when he got put in care,
That's why I hardly go anywhere.
It was my birthday yesterday, I was seven,
I wonder how old I will be when I go up to Heaven.

Danielle Beech (12)
King Edward VI High School, Stafford

As The Snow Falls

The snow is white
So beautiful and calm.
It falls gently on my window ledge
So silent and slow.

It flies with the wind
So swift and gentle
Like a bird in the sky.
This is what I see on a snowy winter's day.

As the snow falls,
I say to myself,
'When will it stop,
I want to go out
On this snowy, winter's day.'

Thomas Fox (12)
King Edward VI High School, Stafford

My Two Little Hamsters!

My two little hamsters,
are my cute little dancers.
They are asleep by day
and awake by night.
The go around and around in their ball,
they're ever so cute and ever so small.

Bubble and Squeak
are ever so meek
but only when they want to sleep
you wouldn't hear a peep.

Abbey Sanders (12)
King Edward VI High School, Stafford

Winter

The snow falls gently to the cold ground
And the wind hums like a hummingbird.
The icicles stay straight and still
And the birds sit in their warm nests.
And your breath turns ice cold,
Your toes go like ice bricks.
I do like winter.

Sam Arnot (12)
King Edward VI High School, Stafford

Away With Words

The world is breaking
Because of the smoke people are making.
When people drive around in their cars
Passing all the bars,
They don't think it's bad,
But when the world disappears they will be sad.
Instead they could be happy here,
Moving, dancing and maybe adults drinking beer.
Every day the world gets worse
If we don't stop now, we will be part of the curse.
So choose what you would like,
To be dead or to see your children ride their bikes.
All the bad air
Runs through your children's hair,
Into their mouths
And into their bodies south.
It could make them die
And the sky will no longer be high
And away will be the birds
But they could just take it away with words.

Louise Hibbett (12)
King Edward VI High School, Stafford

Rainbows

Rainbows are fun for everyone
A pot of gold at the end
Red, yellow, pink, and green
You may enjoy that great big beam
The smile on those children's faces
Spreads joy around this great place
What a beautiful creation
All colours of explosion
Colourful creation.

Jessica Kearns (12)
King Edward VI High School, Stafford

My Dog

M y dog is cute
A lso very old
G oing outside, she comes to your feet
G oing on walks she loves to run
I take her for walks
E xciting to play with.

Sam Davies (12)
King Edward VI High School, Stafford

Away With Words

My pony's white as snow,
He's tall and handsome,
He's got eyes of silver,
He's got a heart of gold.
He's soft as silk,
He's such a gentleman
Just like a prince.
One day he will meet his loving princess.
He's a stunning gelding,
He's as fast as lightning,
He loves me.

Elizabeth Austin (12)
King Edward VI High School, Stafford

Snowflakes

Snow is falling all around me
A beautiful sight to see
I am jumping with glee
As the snowflakes fall on the ground
Children playing, making sounds
As they run all around
Snow is fun for everyone
Once the fluffy snow has gone
Sad because the sun shone.

Chelsea-Marie Martin (12)
King Edward VI High School, Stafford

The Day

The morning starts, a deep blue sky
Stars are out still gleaming by
The human beings rest their heads
Whilst their bodies are still in bed
The sun creeps up
When it wakes up
The bright light shines
Sparkles in eyes
The heat's getting hot
So up they get
Late for work
She's not ready yet
It's now midday
The sun is at its best
Shining proud
With the brightness of its chest
It comes down a little at three o'clock
Then at eight it's down, tick-tock
All is quite silent
All is nearly still
The owl wakes up with a big thrill
The sparkling sky is sparkling through
It's just like morning at half-past two
It is now ten
Goodnight says the hen
Wake you up soon
Way before noon.

Laura Campbell (12)
King Edward VI High School, Stafford

My Dogs

He's tall, she's small,
They both have fur.
He's brown, she's yellow,
They are both healthy.

She's greedy, he's not,
They will never bite,
They've got brown eyes,
They wag their tails
When people arrive.
These are my dogs,
I love them always.
Honey and Max.

Georgie Dias (12)
King Edward VI High School, Stafford

My Life

What's my life about?
Friends and family I suppose,
Jewellery, make-up, money and clothes.
Sometimes it can be a bore,
But when it's great I want more.
What is life about you say?
Just do it your way.

Georgina Lycett (12)
King Edward VI High School, Stafford

Dreams

Two days ago a boy was born,
He looked like a new footballer.
His father bought him a football kit,
People said he would be a brawler.

He grew up into an athletic lad,
And he longed to live his dream.
Quick, strong and brave this boy,
He never ate cookies and cream.

As he got to the age of fourteen
He got scouted by a club.
Now his career had taken to the sky,
Man United the Premiership team.

Another five years had passed,
He developed all of his skills.
Then the manager came along,
And said, 'Your dream's here at last.'

He was given his chance to start,
He took it with open arms.
So he was played as a striker,
People said he played football with an art.

Thirty years ago he was born young and clean,
And now he was a Premiership star.
So that just shows, as a young boy,
Never give up your dream.

Tom Johnson (12)
King Edward VI High School, Stafford

Away With Words

I read a treasure trove
the ink flows and I
zoom through a starry sky.
I float on an ocean
a sea full of waves and words.
Unhurried, flying through my head.
Stays then splashes
in sparkling rays.
Nurturing my mind
I love the stories
and fall into
a world of words.
I am away with words.

Rosie Pettifor (12)
King Edward VI High School, Stafford

To My Baby

Ten tiny fingers,
Ten tiny toes,
Two little eyes
And a button nose.
One little mouth to gurgle and cry,
Two little hands to wave bye-bye,
Two little ears to hear me say,
'You are special in every way!'

Charlotte Baxter (13)
King Edward VI High School, Stafford

Raindrop

I'm falling down from the sky
And I just don't know why.

Plummeting down to the ground
And my buddies are all around.

I see the ground staring up at me,
I knew this was meant to be.

The floor draws ever near
And yet I feel no fear.

I know at last I can rest and lay
I hit the ground - and fade away.

Russell Kingsfield (12)
King Edward VI High School, Stafford

The Poor

Ten years of being poor,
Begging for money.
All my clothes are torn,
The rumbles from my tummy.

Under a tree I beg
For things I don't deserve.
Every fourth person throws me 50p
Today I became £2.50 richer.
In ten years time
How rich will I become?

Natasha Frost (11)
King Edward VI High School, Stafford

A Celebrity

Always smiling for the press,
Loves to wear a flirty dress.
Travelling around in a white shiny limo,
Always in the spotlight.

Never alone,
There are always people.
I'm not saying it's not cool,
Having your own pool.

Sometimes I wish I could be,
A normal person with a normal life
Instead of smiling for the press,
Even though I love my flirty dress.

Jessica Thristan (11)
King Edward VI High School, Stafford

All On My Own

Curled up in a sheet, all alone,
Cold with no water or food.
People staring at my empty hat for money,
I look up at the sky as the pigeons coo.

Families laughing, happy and loved,
While here I am hungry and lost.
I have no fire to keep me warm,
I'm just sitting cold from the frost.

Summer has faded, no more sun,
Winter is approaching, worst time of the year.
Everyone's happy because of the snow,
All is well except me, I won't give a cheer.

Jenny Edwards (12)
King Edward VI High School, Stafford

A Celebrity

Riding around in a limousine,
They always love to be seen.
Always wearing flirty clothes,
Wearing jewellery in their ears and nose.

Always smiling for the press,
Thinking that they are the best.
Owning everything in the shops,
Expensive things down to mops.

Sometimes I wish I were a celeb,
Having my own house,
With my own pool.
Don't you think that would be so cool?

Vicki Peake (11)
King Edward VI High School, Stafford

Thrown Away

T his is me, I am lonely, I have been thrown away.

H e put me in here on my own, I'm hoping he'll come back one day.

R eally, why did they put me in here? I've got no one.

O rphan I am. What have I done?

W ill I ever be loved again? I have no parents so,

N ow what shall I do? Who should I give my love to.

A way in this prison, am I a bad person?

W hat, why and who shall I turn to?

A m I a prisoner? Am I being tested?

Y ou are so lucky that you are loved, but I am in a children's home,

never forget this.

Whitney Stanbra (11)
King Edward VI High School, Stafford

Away With Words!

I'm stuck behind cages
And I'm being watched.
I'm stuck behind cages,
I will show them who's the boss.

I'm stuck behind cages
And I've tried to get out.
I'm stuck behind cages,
Stretching my claws, ready to pounce.

They're watching me,
They're calling me.
What shall I do?
Shall I pounce?
That jeep over there keeps beeping.

Am I really a tiger?
Why am I here?
Where is my jungle?
Why am I stuck here
With those funny things?

Rhianne Brumby-Pattyson (12)
King Edward VI High School, Stafford

Thierry Henry

T he best footballer in the world!

H e can score fantastic goals.

I t's no problem in the box,

E very shot curls into the top corner.

R ed cards he never gets.

R onaldinho is one of his best friends.

Y ears and years of friendship they have.

H e plays for France, 1998, World Cup winners.

E ven if they're losing 1-0 he never gives up.

N ever would he play dirty.

R ed is not his colour.

Y et he is still the best player in the world.

Tom Minshull (12)
King Edward VI High School, Stafford

Why Am I Here?

I often wonder why I'm here.
Is it to feel and live in fear.

The world nowadays has turned evil,
With people all spiteful instead of feeble.

The Third World is in desperate need,
Whereas the West lives in riches and greed.

I often wonder if there's a place for me,
In this world far from harmony.

James Tomkinson (11)
King Edward VI High School, Stafford

Blind Man

Someone walks in
I can't see them,
Just hear them.

They talk to me.
Growing ever wary,
I ask the person who they are,
No answer.

It is no one
I think to myself.
Just the wind.

I call my guide dog,
He comes to me
And all my worries disappear.

Just another sightless day.

James Riach (11)
King Edward VI High School, Stafford

Being Blind

I cannot see.
I suppose that's how God made me.
It's made me strong,
As if I can live long.
It sometimes makes me feel scared,
As if nobody cared.
I walk around with a dog every time I go out.
I feel as if people think, *what's that all about.*

Will I ever be free?

Kelly Marie Nicklin (12)
King Edward VI High School, Stafford

Who Am I?

I scratch at the door
With my sharp claws.
I prowl around at night
With my eyes, they're so very bright.
I purr to get people's attention,
Oh sorry, did I forget to mention
That I love the stuff that comes in tins.
It's funny but I also take a shine to the stuff that comes in bins.

Misha Weston (11)
King Edward VI High School, Stafford

Why Me?

Lying in a cardboard box,
Cold, wet, forgotten.
Crying out to all the world,

Why me?

Snuggling up to my furry tail,
Covering my paws.
Trying to get some rest now.

Why me?

Walking in the freezing cold,
Press my ears down flat.
Something's coming to get me.

Why me?

Warm arms around my tum,
Gently lifting up.
Wrap me in a blanket.

Finally!

Sarah Knight (12)
King Edward VI High School, Stafford

My Wedding

I open my eyes
and then find a
wonderful bride to be.
All colours shining
red and gold
and butterflies flying
with me
gracefully down the aisle.
Flowers twinkling and
lights shining
very strange, bizarre
and with one big breath
I said the words,
'I do!'

Nicole Hewitt (12)
King Edward VI High School, Stafford

That Stupid Child

Every day this happens.
Every day I wish
That this
Was just a dream.
She comes out shouting,
Blames everything on me,
Doesn't explain what I've done.
I just sit there waiting, waiting
For her to . . . !

Every day this happens.
Every day I wish
That this
Was just a dream.
She's so evil
And so mad
I don't feel like living,
It makes me so sad.
I feel like screaming.

Every day this happens,
Every day I wish
That this
Was just a dream.
She needs help,
I need advice,
I don't know what to do,
I feel I do not belong!
Shall I run away?

Hannah Holden (11)
King Edward VI High School, Stafford

The Little Wood Girl

The night before Christmas
people were rushing around
getting the last stock of presents.
Left there all by myself,
no one to love me,
no one to comfort me.
Just me left alone,
me and my cardboard box
filled with chunks of wood.

If only I could sell one
or maybe two or three!
Oh please come and buy one
it'll make my mum proud.
It was getting colder by the minute,
my toes were frozen.
All I ever dream of is sitting by the fire
with food and drink.
Remember! All you have to do
is to buy some of my wood
and maybe my dream will come true.

Chelsey Roberts (12)
King Edward VI High School, Stafford

World Of Wonder

I peeked in through the door.
I stepped in.
My reflection on the floor,
I looked up.
Colours, colours everywhere:
Pink, green, purple, blue,
Yellow, brown, they were all over the place.
I walked in the middle,
I heard a little riddle.
'We're small and sleek,
Smart and weak.
We are real fast
And we like to laugh.
'What are we?'
''Em, 'erm, leprechauns?'
'Congratulations, you have won,
Now be free and have lots of fun!'

Lucy Trumper (11)
King Edward VI High School, Stafford

Heaven I'm In

H ere I lie
E ven though I don't know how I died
A nd people are sad that I am dead
V ery sad I lost my head.
E mma is my name
N o one takes the blame.

I 'm crying, missing my mom,
M y age is but one.

I 'm never going to live again
N ow I'm not in pain.

Jack Heywood (12)
King Edward VI High School, Stafford

On A Cloud

I am white mist
floating in the sky
over the ground
every day.

I stay awake
thinking about steak.
I need a rest
but I am a big mess.

I wish I was one of them
to have some food
then a little drink
for this cloud.

I travel all day
on one pair of feet.
I am a cloud.

Christian Masterson (12)
King Edward VI High School, Stafford

Pete The Postman

My name is Pete
And I go to the beat,
I am a postman
And my mates call me John.
I go to school
And I act like a fool.
I deliver to King Eddie's High School.

Jake Higgott (12)
King Edward VI High School, Stafford

My Dog

I am small and furry,
I have big blue eyes,
I am brown and white,
I am sometimes really greedy,
I will never bite,
Always lively when people arrive.

I am the best dog ever.

Katie Tunnicliffe (12)
King Edward VI High School, Stafford

Climbing

I love to climb trees
It is my hobby.
When I reach the top
I can feel the breeze.
I even climb when there is nobody there
And I climb with my friend.
I like to climb trees
And love to get to the end.

Jordan Riley (12)
King Edward VI High School, Stafford

Florida

I woke up at three in the morning,
A couple of hours before the sun was dawning.
Packing the suitcases, ready to go,
Shall we pack jumpers? No, no, no!

We are going on the plane ready to fly,
Going 5,000ft into the sky.
My stomach tosses and turns
I feel like the engine is ready to burn.

As we are landing
We are going round and round
My heart is getting
Ready to bound.

We go to the hotel and finally to bed,
Bang, bang, bang, went my head.
I huddle under the duvet
Finally I was going to bed.

Samantha Exley (12)
King Edward VI High School, Stafford

Top Midfielder

Running down the line with the ball,
scoring for Liverpool.
It is so cool.
Cross the ball in the box,
I take a couple of knocks,
mud on my socks.
I strike the ball at the goal,
it skims the pole.
The crowd roars,
one-nil we win.

Connor Davies (12)
King Edward VI High School, Stafford

Child Abuse

My name is Sarah, I am but three,
My eyes are swollen, I cannot see.
I must be stupid, I must be bad,
What else could have made my daddy so mad?
I wish I were better, I wish I weren't ugly,
Then maybe my mummy would still want to hug me.
I can't speak, I can't do wrong,
Or else I'm locked up all day long.
The house is dark, my folks aren't home,
When my mummy comes home I try to be nice
So I only get one whipping tonight.
I don't make a sound, I just heard a car,
Dad's back from Charlie's Bar.
I hear him curse, my name he calls,
I press myself against the walls.
I try to hide from his evil eyes,
I'm afraid and now I start to cry.
Whipping me, he shouts ugly words,
He says it's my fault he suffers at work.
He slaps me and hits me and yells at me more
I'm finally free, I run for the door.
My name is Sarah, I'm only three,
Tonight my daddy murdered me.

Deana McEleny (12)
King Edward VI High School, Stafford

Day And Night

The sky is blue,
The sun and sky were stuck like glue.
The sun went down,
I did nothing but frown.
Moon glowing in the dark,
Dogs just bark.
I heard a noise,
It was just those noisy boys.

The morning struck,
As I was reading my book.
The sun shone all day,
The waves were calm, down by the bay.
The day had started and ended.

Amber Harrison (12)
King Edward VI High School, Stafford

Shoots And Scores

Should I hit the ball from the halfway line?
But I have only got a little time.
Should I run to the box with it
Or should I pass it a bit?
There's a man to my left and a man to my right,
But there's a man coming to me, it is going to be tight.
I take him on
But then comes another one.
I pass it to Joe Ford
He shoots and he scores.

Ashley Burton (12)
King Edward VI High School, Stafford

Bugatti Veyron

B rilliant performance
U nusual power
G reat speed
A wesme interior
T otally terrific
T echnically tasteful
I mpressive exterior.

V ibrant colours
E xtra impressive
Y ippee hooray
R ocking all around
O bvioiusly cool
N otoriously excellent.

William Venables (12)
King Edward VI High School, Stafford

My House

M y house is a great place to live.
Y ou could come and live with me.

H ow would you like that?
O utside I have a beautiful huge garden.
U p in the roof top is a dusty old attic.
S oft sofas and chairs to lounge in.
E veryone likes chilling out at my place.

Ben James (11)
King Edward VI High School, Stafford

Here At The Stables

H ere at the stables,
O n my pony I will ride,
R iding into the sunset,
S ometimes cold and sometimes hot,
E ver going,
S traw for their bedding.
　　　　All for Poppy, Annie, Chelsea and Flint.

P ony riding,
O nce again,
N ever ending,
I n the paddock, jumping and cantering,
E quine animals,
S how jumping dressage and fun rides.

Amber Hill (11)
King Edward VI High School, Stafford

New York

A New York Yankees' ball hits my head,
I can see the Statue of Liberty from my hotel bed.
I grab a yellow taxi to take me down town,
The lights of Times Square sparkle like a crown.
I step out of Macy's collaged in bags,
I've got lots of bargains, you can check the tags.
Buildings everywhere, both big and small,
Thousands of celebs pouring out of a fabulous ball.
This is the place to be,
Can't you see?
New York!

Rebecca Crowe (11)
King Edward VI High School, Stafford

Away With Words

Creeping, stalking,
Pouncing, hiding.

Slobbering, dripping,
Listening, smelling.

Eyeing, touching,
Playing, torturing.

Gritting, biting,
Woofing, snarling.

I've got it, the dog food.

Luke Emery (11)
King Edward VI High School, Stafford

Tamarli

T errifying teeth that could kill you
A wareness is needed at all times!
M ischievious like a little tyke
A mazingly beautiful soft skin
R avenously hungry all the time
L eaping through the green grass
I love him very much and nothing can change that.

Harley Andow-Giles (11)
King Edward VI High School, Stafford

Creatures

Searching through the jungle, for something yummy to eat,
He squelches, squelches, squelches, as mud sticks to his feet.
Squelching, squelching, squelching,
Squelching scorpions.

Crawling along the beach, heading for the open land,
He seems to be struggling, as his feet sink in the sand.
Crawling, crawling, crawling,
Crawling crabs.

Swimming through the salty sea, stinging human beings,
He's drowning really fast, whilst people lose their feelings.
Stinging, stinging, stinging,
Stinging jellyfish.

Spinning webs on windowpanes, creeping, crawling around,
He's moving really fast, whilst people frighten and frown.
Spinning, spinning, spinning,
Spinning spiders.

Sarah Wilde (11)
King Edward VI High School, Stafford

Best Friends

B e there for each other
E ncourage each other
S tick together
T ell each other secrets.

F eelings for each other
R ely on each other
I couldn't do without them
E xplain each other's views
N urse each other if we're down
D efinitely great
S eriously best friends.

Kayleigh Hill (11)
King Edward VI High School, Stafford

Shopping

S hopping is the best
H oping my mum will pay for my new shoes
O h what can I buy?
P ink shoes
P ink handbags
I ncredible is my mum, paying for it all!
N ew clothes on the way
G o shopping!

Joelle Lock (11)
King Edward VI High School, Stafford

Away With The Words

Higher than birds, the words they fly,
Whole flocks of them in the sky.
I see them above the aeroplanes
Like bumblebees gone insane.

Away with words,
Across the sea,
Over Paris and cities high.
That's the way the words fly,
That's the way the words fly.

If pigs could fly, I'm sure I could too,
The crows fly high,
Yet the words
Overhead shout, 'Boo!'
The flocks swarm
Over cold and warm.

Away with words,
Across the sea,
Over Paris and cities high.
That's the way the words fly,
That's the way the words fly high!

Sophie Lowndes (12)
King Edward VI High School, Stafford

The Seasons

All the seasons of the world,
long, short warm or cold.
Day by day the seasons take us through the years,
watching people getting old.
Each one has its own personality.
Winter, cold with freezing nights.
Autumn, frosty with lots of frights.
Summer, boiling, burning all day long,
Spring, lambs leaping about.
The four seasons
They're alright!

Rachel Perry (11)
King Edward VI High School, Stafford

My Cat Monty

His coat shimmers in the sun,
He has handsome hazel eyes,
His whiskers are like delicate thread webs,
He has beautiful orangey stripes.
My cat Monty.

He's kind and caring,
He's fierce and brave,
He's gentle and cuddly,
He's clever and thoughtful.
My cat Monty.

His steps are light,
His run is powerful,
His leaps are magnificent,
He's faster than a cheetah.
My cat Monty.

He lies lazily in the sun,
He pounces silently on his prey,
He laps up milk energetically,
He plays enthusiastically.
My cat Monty.

Rachel Winnington (12)
King Edward VI High School, Stafford

Friends

F rinds are the best things you can have.

R eally kind, really friendly and always there for a laugh.

I ndoors or outdoors they always want to play.

E veryone needs friends.

N ine, ninety or nine hundred, you never have too many friends.

D an, Calum or Ryan, they all have different names.

S ad or happy, your friends will always be there.

Josh Greenway (12)
King Edward VI High School, Stafford

My Lil' Dog

My dog is the cutest ever
But smart, he is never.
He chases shadows and light,
He's given me a bit of a bite.
Almost put down,
I persuaded Dad not to.
If he had I would have given him a frown.
I almost gave my dad a shock
My lil' dog will never go
If he ever does I will know
Whoever does it will be sorry.
Even more if they watch Corrie.

Liam Edwards (11)
King Edward VI High School, Stafford

Heaven

I believe in a place
So far from here.
This place is Heaven,
I wonder what it's like up there?
Is it white or gold,
Pink or blue?
I wonder if there're angels up there too
Or is that just another dream waiting to come true?
Is the grass always green
And the sky always blue?
Is love always pure
And hatred not heard of?

Jade Lowe (11)
King Edward VI High School, Stafford

When I'm Away With The Words

When I'm away with the words,
I can be anywhere but still be here.
I can go back in time, hear things I shouldn't hear.
When I can face my worst fear,
I know I'm away with the words,
In a fantasy world of my own.

When I'm away with the words,
I'm in total control,
I can fly up high with the birds.
When I can run by the fastest wild herd,
I know I'm away with the words
In a distant world of my own.

When I'm away with the words,
I can see the fairies dancing by,
I can run with them and dance with them.
When I can ride on a rhino's back without being condemned,
I know I'm away with the words,
In a magical world of my own.

Anna Welch (11)
King Edward VI High School, Stafford

Away With Words

Out of the corner of my eye,
I glimpse a balloon high in the sky.
I wish I could be in that place,
Where the air is still and full of grace.
And words once spoken flutter down,
Landing so softly on the ground.
It bobs and curtseys to and fro,
Watching over the people below.
My thoughts are streaming,
Am I dreaming?
Silence reigns . . .
Away with words.

Ella Wood (11)
King Edward VI High School, Stafford

Low - Haiku

Crime it never pays,
Staring at the judge, waiting.
Guilty, the worst word.

Wade Sorrensen (11)
King Edward VI High School, Stafford

Lucy

She is ahead of me,
What today? Go on you choose.
Jumping around together, always smiling.
I'm bored but she comes quick.
You're drifting away, where are you?
You're gone, disappeared into thin air.
I will miss you so much,
I will remember the good times,
But she has left me now,
Never to come back.

Nadine Turner (12)
King Edward VI High School, Stafford

My Gerbil Pepper

G obbling on dried food and treats
E xcited when let loose
R unning like a mad thing in her cage
B oundless energy, it never ends
I mpressive amount of energy
L oveable, sweet round face.

P erfect companions are gerbils
E veryone different and sweet
P erfectly playful but can be pongy
P epper ticks every one of these
E xcitable, enchanting,
R eally faithful, but Pepper sometimes escapes.

Charlotte Dawson (11)
King Edward VI High School, Stafford

Toby

T abby and taut, well knows where he's going
O pens his eyes like white clean dishes and they are
                                 as bright as a shining torch.
B eing quite lazy, doesn't move much.
Y ou know when he's around because of the noise he makes,
                               thumping and bumping and crashing.

Steven Wilson (11)
King Edward VI High School, Stafford

Homework For High School

'H ello,' says the teacher.

' I 'm here,' say I

'G ot my homework for

H istory today

S orry Miss though, I forgot my maths

C at scratched it to pieces

H owever half I retrieved

O h but it had weed on that

O h but I did my science today

L ost my planner so couldn't do the rest.'

Emma Price (11)
King Edward VI High School, Stafford

Winter

W inds getting stronger,
 I cy waters,
N estling birds,
T ime to get ready,
E veryone's excited,
R obins are singing softly.
 Winter's here and Santa's getting ready.

Sarah Turner (11)
King Edward VI High School, Stafford

Football Kennings

Crowd roaring
Keepers prancing
Friend making
Grass greening
Fun growing
Line flagging
Fans cheering
Post rattling
Great finishing
Gooaall!

Chris Marsden (11)
King Edward VI High School, Stafford

Girls

We do our make-up and our hair,
But do we even have a care?
Like the things that bore us most
Especially when people boast and boast.
You know the thing we like the most,
It's boys, it's boys, they're our host.

We have parties nearly every night
We go to town without a fright.
We love to shop, it's so cool,
I love every shop, they all rule.
All us girls have the same brain,
We know when it's going to rain.
I hope you enjoyed my poem so,
But now I have to go.

Paris Roberts (12)
King Edward VI High School, Stafford

Christmas Is Here

Winter is here,
There's snow everywhere,
Little Robin Redbreast is flying all around,
Children getting ready for Santa to come,
Christmas is here,
Christmas is here.

Chloe Plant ((12)
King Edward VI High School, Stafford

The Answer To A Child's Question

Have you ever wondered
what floats upon the sea?
Have you ever thought
about the wonders you could see?
Everybody knows about
other people's thoughts,
but do they really believe
the first things they were taught.

Do you ever think about
what you're going to say?
Do you ever dream about what
adventures come next day?
Will you ever kill or fight,
and stalk around at night?
Now that's the answer to a child's question.

Loren Matthews (11)
King Edward VI High School, Stafford

A Fruit's Life

Apples in a tree,
Tomatoes from the ground,
Fruit and veg are waiting,
Ready to be found.

Bananas in a cupboard,
Pears in a bowl,
Into your mouth,
A giant, scary hole.

Going in the stomach,
(not the best thing)
Down to the intestine
(not a great theme).

Finally we're coming out,
I see a bright shiny light
But suddenly we fall,
Into a strange liquid.
Jeepers, what a fright.

Very soon we're floating,
Staying very calm,
Then the waterfalls start up
I hope it cannot harm.

James Rounds (11)
King Edward VI High School, Stafford

Teachers

My best teacher is Mr Camm
He is very funny.
Then it's Mrs Vincent
Whose smile makes it sunny.

Now it's Mr Holgeth,
He is cool for what he does.
Next it's Miss Trimmings
Who makes us do our best.

Next it's Mr Dance,
Oh, it is great.
Last but not least Mr Christy
Science on a plate.

So they're all my favourite teachers
Hope you like them too.

Thomas Webb (11)
King Edward VI High School, Stafford

Homeless

I ran away from home at the age of eleven,
because I hate my life!
Hate my parents, school, everything.
I found a small porchway, I now call my home
In the middle of town,
And I nicked a trolley I now call my room.

With only £50 I stole from my parents for food,
I am getting weaker and weaker,
I am so lonely on my own day in, day out,
I cry myself to sleep with the energy I have left.

I am terrified of what is to come next,
I am so cold, I cannot feel my toes,
I am so scared, I can't sleep at night,
I pray for the next day to be better.

All I wear is a tattered old blanket, with thin trousers and a T-shirt,
My shoes are so small, my toes are poking out and I get
enormous blisters.
I see people walking past with delicious burgers, I wish I had one.
People walk past waving their money around, sometimes I
get the urge to steal it, but I just can't.

Calum Ferguson (11)
King Edward VI High School, Stafford

Liverpool Fans

L oyal to the team,
I nvolved and interested in Liverpool,
V ast haters of Everton,
E nthralled with The Kop, the crowd, the glory,
R oped to The Shankley Gates,
P erplexed by the icy fingers of defeat,
O n cloud nine with victory!
O nce a fan, always a fan!
L overs of the Liverbird.

F aithful and dedicated,
A ddicted to Anfield's atmosphere,
N ever giving up on the players,
S ingers of 'You'll Never Walk Alone'.

Sam Lloyd (11)
King Edward VI High School, Stafford

Away With Words

Open your eyes,
Open your mind,
Open the door of imagination.

Find your feet,
Fight your fear,
Write it down; keep it near.

Words that smile,
Words that cry,
Words that tell a story; what happened and why.

Away with words - let your pen fly
To the land of ink and paper; I think it's nearby.

Look in the dictionary for inspiration,
It's got helping hands for alliteration.

Words that are used and words that are not,
Words from the future and words past - forgot.

Onomatopoeia - a word hard to spell,
Transforms your story like the *bong* of a bell.

Away with words, a train of thought,
Unlock your mind with the key you were taught.

Think up rhymes,
Think of love,
Any topic perhaps from above.

Grammar, punctuation, adjectives and nouns,
Speech, conjunctions - your writing knows no bounds,
Mix them in a recipe a spectacular make.

Away with words a very special bake.

In your head, your heart and your soul,
Find your safe of imagination and make it whole.

Luck and wisdom, words and ink
Write them down, you just need to think.

Just play away with words.

Hannah Bevington (12)
King Edward VI High School, Stafford

I'm A Pencil

I'm a pencil
Sharpened to the sharpest point,
To write and to be drawn with,
I'm held in your hand.

I'm used to drawing shapes,
I'm used to drawing angles,
I'm used to underlining,
I'm used most of the time.

I like my friend, the ruler,
Helps me draw straight,
I underline the title,
And sometimes the date.

I love being a pencil,
It's fun and I'm always used,
I love my friend, the ruler,
As best mates, together we're fused.

Josie Blenheim (12)
King Edward VI High School, Stafford

Finish It . . .

I walked down the dusty road,
It was dark, cold and had a wet atmosphere.
With my hood up, feeling sorry for myself.
I felt like death had come and hit me in the face.
The old flashing lamppost was my home,
I curled up in a ball.
I thought, *at least this will be the last night of the nightmare I'm living.*
I sat and prayed to God, explaining my feelings.
I grabbed the small black machine out of my pocket,
One shot . . . it was time!

Juliet Shaw (12)
King Edward VI High School, Stafford

The Summer!

Rays of sunlight gleaming down at us,
Shining brightly, warming up the grateful people far, far below,
But this beautiful ball of light could also be a lethal weapon,
Burning us, blinding us,
The harmful rays could ruin our lives,
And all because we wanted a tan . . .

Laura Heeley (12)
King Edward VI High School, Stafford

Cat Life

Cats big and small
All different shapes and sizes
Tackling life with incredible experience
Away with speed and strength
Snow leopards, lions, panthers and house cats
Each gifted with beauty and fun
Patterns and textures
All different colours
Silky, soft, furry and thick
All happy and joyful
Filled with love
Stripy and spotty, plain and cute
They take pride in loving their kittens
Full of love!

Zoe Bright (12)
King Edward VI High School, Stafford

Darkness Is . . .

(Inspired by Rachel Smith)

Darkness is velvet
Darkness is black
Darkness is night
Darkness is a black cat
Darkness is nothingness
Darkness is the world without a light on.

Light is the sun
Light is the day sky
Light is a baby's smile
Light is the world with a candle lit
Light is a white cat
Light is God's grace.

Ellie Smith (12)
King Edward VI High School, Stafford

War

So close to death,
You can taste it in the air.
These people have looked death in the eyes,
But turned away,
And carried on fighting,
Fighting for their country.
Grief of a mother,
Her little boy has gone,
But joy for a family,
Their relative is home again.
Honour, Courage, Bravery.

Sophie Clay (12)
King Edward VI High School, Stafford

Shadows

They follow you everywhere,
Every time you look, they are there.
They can make you look plump,
They can make you look thin and skinny.
They can make you look tall,
And make you look short.
Their looks can be deceiving,
Their looks can be frightening.
Sometimes you can mistake trees
For monsters and ghosts.
Sometimes you can mistake teddy bears
For wild beasts.
Some people say that shadows
Are just your body blocking the light.
That's a lie!
Shadows are people,
Like us in every way.
They adapt to one person,
Sometimes they stay and
Sometimes they stray away.
My shadow will not leave me alone.

Rebecca Johnson (12)
King Edward VI High School, Stafford

Away With Words

The wind blowing through my hair,
The rain dripping on my face as I sat there waiting.
Waiting for him to come.
Then I blinked.

There he was,
Black clothes,
Pale-faced,
Scrunched fists,
As he walked closer.

The blood was dripping from my mouth,
Red marks over my face, arms and body;
Then my eyes shut.

Sam Newbold (12)
King Edward VI High School, Stafford

Blind

Black, black, everywhere,
A blanket of darkness,
Light has long left me,
No one to talk to, to see,
I only feel, hear, talk and smell,
My touch, now my vital sense,
To find my way around.

Charlotte Deall (12)
King Edward VI High School, Stafford

Football

F iring up the fans
O pposition are going mad
O h, it's a goal!
T he sound from the fans is ecstatic
B elief in your team
A ll the seats are packed
L ively fans
L oving the win!

Shaun Gibbs (11)
King Edward VI High School, Stafford

On The Ice

Blind and helpless I stumbled along.
Waiting a minute, it can't be long
Five long minutes, I waited in suspense,
Something was going on, I knew, I could sense.
Finally the time had come
To take off my blindfold, I thought they would run.
But no, they all stayed right where they were,
Shouted, 'Surprise!'
But then not a stir.
Except shouts of excitement, and then to occur
Was the hustle and bustle to get to the rink
To go ice skating and get food and drink.
Whizzing round the ice like a leopard on skates,
I had been around ten times, in front of my mates.
But then we had to come away -
I'm going to do this again next birthday.

Kezia Purslow (11)
King Edward VI High School, Stafford

Fabulous Tricks

The show begins,
The curtains are lifted,
First up, clowns flip and trip,
Lights sparkle and twinkle,
Men and women shoot through moving hoops.
People do roly-polys on a piece of string,
Clowns try to do flips on ropes but trip,
Elephants dance and bounce,
Next come stilt walkers and talkers
Tricks and flips.
Last of all the presenter of the show.
Then laughs and coughs and presents
The end of the show.

Katherine Key (12)
King Edward VI High School, Stafford

The Weather

It's going to rain,
I hate it because it's such a pain,
It overflows the drains,
That's why it's such a pain.

It's supposed to snow on Christmas Day,
I hope it does, so I can play.
If it doesn't snow I will play with my new toys,
And have my mates around so everyone enjoys.

Sam Booth (12)
King Edward VI High School, Stafford

Away With Words

Sun's shining, scorching hot,
Sand's burning people's feet
Running quickly to the sea,
Children making sculptures.

Sea's clear,
See straight under,
People splashing, having fun,
Adults sunbathing, hoping to get a tan,
Everyone having a nap.

Molly Stowe (12)
King Edward VI High School, Stafford

Away With Words

Away with words!
Away with words?
How can I go away with words?

I saw a way,
I know a way
To go away with words?

This place I saw
Too wonderful for me
To describe in words!

But I will try,
I really will try,
To describe this place in words!

Great blue seas
And bright green peas
Are in this place of words!

Light sandy beaches,
And lovely ripe peaches
Are in this place of words!

Homes galore
For rich and poor
Are in this place of words!

Rugby, cricket, football,
Tennis 'n' all
Are in this place of words!

Pop music tones,
And rock music moans
Are in this place of words!

The royal family's cool
And the Prime Minister rules,
In this place of words!

This place I say,
Is the UK
And that's this place of words!

Isaac Alcock (12)
King Edward VI High School, Stafford

I Lost You, So Everyone Has To Lose Me

I'm sitting here all alone,
ashamed to say depressed.
I wish I was under a headstone
instead I am so stressed.

Tears of blood roll down my face,
as I move the blade towards my wrist.
Soon I will be in a happy place,
but unlikely to be missed.

I miss him more than words can say,
need him back into my arms.
Every day I used to pray,
and no longer will our hands join palms.

He left me on that cold Christmas Eve,
I felt so empty, so dark and numb.
The only thing I have done is grieve,
I cannot believe what's he's made me become.

Day and night, his name is in my head,
memories of the happiness stick.
All the time I wish I was dead,
Why I don't know but I'm still lovesick.

After tonight I shall not feel empty, dark or numb,
no longer will I have to grieve.
I will have nothing to do with what has to come,
because soon my life I have to leave.

Jessica Cope (16)
Sir Thomas Boughey High School, Stoke-on-Trent

Erpgore

Poor Erpgore, the monster down the lane,
He was so lonely but no one felt his pain.
When he went to school, children laughed aloud
And wouldn't let him join in the 'cool crowd'.
They poured water over him and poked him too,
Poor Erpgore didn't know what to do.
But one rainy day when he walked down the lane -
To his surprise, the fairy godmother came!
She waved her wand and guess what she did?
She made the children's cruel words get rid.
And she made poor Erpgore a carnivore -
No more bullies - now that's for sure!
Forever happy Erpgore.

Naomi Marfleet Lakin (11)
Sir Thomas Boughey High School, Stoke-on-Trent

I Wish Writing Poems Was Simple!

'It really is simple,' explained the teacher,
Trying not to sound like a preacher.

'All you need is a pen and some paper!
And don't let your imagination taper!'

So off I went all the way home
To write the poem all on my own.

I got my pen and put it to paper,
writing a poem is a right old caper!

I tried in vain to think of a subject,
But everything I did ended as a reject.

It dawned on me at last
That I could write a poem, but not very fast.

It may be short and not very good,
But I have done it on my own and didn't think I could!

Thomas Turley (11)
Thomas Telford School, Telford

Will I Come Back Alive?

Watching and waiting
Whilst the clock ticked by,
My time was nearly out.
Sitting and staring,
My mind so blank,
Like I couldn't even remember how to count.

Here I go,
I hope I survive
This roller-coaster I'm about to ride.
There's no turning back,
No going home,
My heart shrivelled up as if I'd died.

On I go,
Climbing aboard,
Sitting down still on my seat.
The blur going by,
My feelings mixed up
About the people I'm about to meet.

Searching around
With a bag that was bulging,
My back aching enormously.
Following the herd
Like a complete stranger,
Looking like I was lost, obviously.

As time flew by
It was nearly over,
I'd soon feel free and cool.
A smile on my face,
I could say I'd survived
My first day at secondary school!

Phoebe Calloway (12)
Thomas Telford School, Telford

Hallowe'en

In the darkness, I'm walking all alone.
My pace I quicken, eager to get home.
Out of the corner of my eye I see a glint of light,
As I turn to look, I get an awful fright,
For there looking at me is a face, big and round,
I try to scream but can't make a sound.
Wizards and witches with bats on long strings,
Goblins and demons, black cats and elves,
I think they are all scary then I look at myself.
A long black cape is my attire,
Yes, you've guessed it . . . I'm a vampire.
The most peculiar street you have ever seen.
Well, what do you expect? It's Hallowe'en!

Jennifer West (11)
Thomas Telford School, Telford

The Surf

Calmly, slowly, rolling, growing,
Building up its strength.
Stronger, taller, faster, wider,
Building up suspense.

Nearly here now, heart beats faster,
One, two, three.
Jump on board for the ride of a lifetime,
You can't keep up with me.

Gushing, swirling, breathless, tingling,
Travelling with the greatest speed.
Crashing, frothing, fizzing, bubbling,
Another go is what I need.

Jake Swan (11)
Thomas Telford School, Telford

I Once Had A Dog Called Business

I once had a dog called Business
His silky fur shone in the light
And when he stared, his eyes shone bright.

I once had a dog called Business
All day he jumped and bounced around
Until he was tired and fell to the ground.

I once had a dog called Business
His tail wagged whenever he saw me
Without a doubt he adored me.

I once had a dog called Business
A smile on my face whenever I saw him
Without a doubt I adored him.

I once had a dog called Business
The way his eyes shone in the dark.
I loved him with all my heart.

Edie Harris (12)
Thomas Telford School, Telford

My Perfect (Imaginary) Sister

She's ecstatic, unique, special in every way possible,
No one knows me as well as her.
The screwed-up faces I make,
She knows what they all mean!

Smart, funny and stylish, she enjoys messing around
And she is always up to mischief!
Pulling pranks on the family!
Yeah, that sounds about right!

She's always there for me,
If it's for a laugh or a shoulder to cry on.
She's always there.
Rain or shine.

When I sit down and think about it,
My *real* sister is like this anyway . . .

Daniella Nicholls (12)
Thomas Telford School, Telford

Dance

I hear the sounds
Of my tap shoes
Tap, tap, tapping
Along the floor
Loud and bold, like a lion's roar.

Pointed feet and tutus
Gliding along the floor
A cute boy on the sidelines
Going, 'Give me
More, more, more!'

Listen to the beat as it moves along
Bang, bang, it's a funky song
All of you come and jump along
Hop and skip
As we move along.

Number 1 has just been on
But now it's me and the rest's to come
On goes the make-up
Up goes the hair
Which is long and fair
On goes the costume and on goes me.

The music is loud
And my singing has made me proud
I entertain the crowd
As they applaud
Really loud.

**Emily Crewe (11), Lauren Pestana,
Lauren Ramkin & Rebecca Flynn**
Thomas Telford School, Telford

Autumn Days

Autumn leaves glow like gold,
Acorns fall from nearby oak trees,
Squirrels gather secret stashes,
Leaves twirl in the gentle breeze.

Hallowe'en is nearby too,
So have you got your pumpkins ready?
Dressing up is such a laugh,
Vampire kids look really deadly.

Hats and scarves come from cupboards,
Gloves to keep your fingers cosy,
Fireworks sparkle like precious gems,
Emeralds, sapphires, rubies rosy.

Looking forward to getting home,
Sitting, eating by the fire,
Just relaxing in the warm,
Sparks climbing higher and higher!

Catherine Hutchinson (11)
Thomas Telford School, Telford

Autumn Leaves

The rustling leaves on the ground
Make a sort of rustling sound,
Leaves that blow from the tree,
Making a pile as high as me.

Like a piece of paper falling down,
In a pile it drowns.
Invisible, which one could it be?
Watch them at home and you will see.

Rebekah Jeffries (11)
Thomas Telford School, Telford

Hallowe'en

Hallowe'en, a festival,
A really scary thing,
With trick or treaters everywhere,
You don't know what to think.

With witches, skeletons,
Pumpkins and beasts,
Knocking on your door
And saying, 'Trick or treat.'

Hallowe'en comes every year
On the 31st of October,
Beware, my friends,
You're in for a scare.

Nicole Carr (12)
Thomas Telford School, Telford

My Faithful Friend

Liver and white,
Got good sight,
My faithful friend.

Chases a ball,
Comes when you call,
My faithful friend.

Soft and sweet,
Licks your feet,
My faithful friend.

Wags her tail,
Brings in your mail,
My faithful friend.

Doesn't moan,
Likes a bone,
My faithful friend.

My faithful friend
Is my dog, Bouncer,
Oh what a faithful friend.

Daisy Clifford (11)
Thomas Telford School, Telford

Giraffe

G azing black eyes shimmer in the sun,
 I n the trees its head lies munching and crunching,
R eaching high, reaching low, its neck goes to and fro,
A patchwork pattern of colours it has,
F earing nothing, it stands elegantly tall,
F acing the dry and golden dusty lands,
E verywhere and anywhere the giraffe is allowed to roam.

Shannon Finnigan (12)
Thomas Telford School, Telford

My Brother, Ben

He's a:
Bedroom messer,
Mum stresser,
Hair puller,
Biscuit lover,
Attention seeker,
Pant leaker,
Spider-Man wannabe,
Hates cuddling me,
Football player,
Monster slayer,
Sweet eater,
Game cheater,
Toy breaker,
Tear faker,
Four years old,
Never does as he's told,
Hides in his den,
My brother, Ben.

Lauren Jones (11)
Thomas Telford School, Telford

Leaves

Leaves are crimson, leaves are gold,
Leaves hang from trees so bold,
Until autumn when they fall to the ground,
Silent they are, they make no sound.

As they fall upon the ground,
Lots of children mill around,
For they know as through them they bustle,
Those silent leaves, they will start to rustle.

Parents watch as children play,
The sun shines brightly this autumn day,
Sounds of laughter fill the air,
Children playing together without a care.

Carpets of orange, red and gold,
Leaves are green, isn't that what we're told?
Yet beneath all of those children's feet,
Those bright autumn leaves shine a treat.

As the sun fades and the wind takes a hold,
The fun-filled day starts to get cold,
Parents and children head off home for tea,
The leaves that fell swirl beneath their tree.

Joshua Bowdley (12)
Thomas Telford School, Telford

The Snake

Waiting in the grass,
Quiet, patient and still,
Until his prey is finally here,
He moves in for the kill.

With a bite filled with venom,
This prey is now his,
The snake swallows it up whole
And gives a satisfied hiss.

When his belly is full,
He slithers off to bed,
Until the time comes again
When he needs to be fed.

Thomas Knowles (11)
Thomas Telford School, Telford

First Day Of School!

I walked to the coach,
Not knowing anyone there,
Seeing all different faces
Was a real big scare.

We got to the school gate,
The coach went in,
I went to my first lesson,
My head started to spin.

But then someone else,
Feeling just the same,
Came up to me at break time
And told me her name.

The next day at school
Wasn't really as bad,
Because now I have friends,
I don't feel so sad.

So when the new Year 7s
Arrive in school,
I'll go and give them comfort
And tell them school is cool!

Robyn Whitehouse (11)
Thomas Telford School, Telford

Autumn Poem

The autumn fall begins,
The leaves are turning brown,
The winds are blowing strong,
The mist is all around.

The birds are no longer singing,
The rain is falling hard,
The soft morning dew,
The ground is damp below.

Hallowe'en is scary but fun,
The children dressing up,
Enjoying trick or treat,
The fireworks aglow as they shoot up
In the night air.

The nights are getting dark,
The moon so bright in the sky,
The people snug and warm,
The winter is on its way.

Peter Swift (11)
Thomas Telford School, Telford

Autumn

Autumn is my favourite season,
And this is for a good reason.
Autumn means Christmas is near,
Which fills us children with great cheer.

The sky is filled with autumn dew,
It feels like the world is brand new,
Nothing beats autumn dew,
Just think of autumn dew.

Autumn is wetter,
Autumn is colder,
Autumn is foggier,
Autumn is wetter, colder and foggier.

The colours of the leaves are bright,
The colours of the trees are a beautiful sight all right,
The colours of the day are bright like the moonlight,
The colours at autumn change.

The days get shorter,
The nights get longer,
The days get colder,
The nights get darker.

Summer is gone,
Winter is near,
Spring is a memory,
Autumn is here.

Kieran Baker (11)
Thomas Telford School, Telford

Autumn Leaves

Leaves are falling to the ground,
Russets, reds and orangey-browns.
They twist and twirl, swirling around,
Floating majestically, without a sound.

A rainbow-coloured carpet
To look at is a pleasure,
Squirrels scampering softly,
Gathering golden treasure.

For winter is almost here.

Simon Harrison (11)
Thomas Telford School, Telford

The Autumn Leaves

They soar like birds in the sky
And can be as brown as the brownest wood.
Their points stick out like small knives,
Or can be smoother than a silk quilt.

They brush your face at high speeds,
Controlled by the muscley and very strong wind.
They come from something so big and tall
And can be a tiny part, but add all the extra to it.

Their vibrant colours scream at you,
It's dull just to say hello,
But they are all just one thing
That I see every day.

Connor Graham (11)
Thomas Telford School, Telford

Cats

Cats are small and furry,
With small little white paws,
With adorable little pink noses,
Who wouldn't want one?
'Not me!' shouted my sister.
'Why?' I asked.
'They can scratch you and bite you
And make a real mess!'
But it would be nice
To have my furry friend at home
For all the best!
We would never have mice,
We would always have company if we were bored.
'So what do you think, Mum?
Can I have a cat?'
'No!'

Jaskiran Deol (12)
Thomas Telford School, Telford

The Autumn

Leaves of gold came tumbling down
To a dewy coat of grass,
The blistering cold froze the plants solid,
The ice-kissed flowers died slowly
And dropped to the ground.
The sun came out and shone around
And restored life to this town.

Josh Morby (11)
Thomas Telford School, Telford

Autumn

Autumn is a period of time,
A changing time,
A strange time,
Watching leaves fall to the ground,
Crane flies and insects, no longer frequently found,
The darkening nights,
The conker fights,
Holidays become part of the past,
Central heating starts to blast,
Autumn, the poor relation it will always be,
To the summer sun and the Christmas tree.

Lucy Squires (11)
Thomas Telford School, Telford

The Match

Yes, shoot, the keeper saves
Cross, head, it hits the post
Bounce, bounce the keeper gathers it up
Chest, shoot, I missed an open goal

Roll, roll, I miss-kicked the ball
Spinning wildly I fall to the ground
Run, sprint, I was too slow
Trying hard but it doesn't seem to work

My heart's thumping like a boxer in the ring
My kit's dirty, I'm soaking wet
Feeling down, need one to win
Come on lads only two minutes to go

The ball is played over the top
Knee volley it's the final attempt
Goal!
I scored at last
Whooooo the crowd goes wild
Champions again, we lift the cup!

Jamie King (12)
Thomas Telford School, Telford

Winter

It's cold outside, crisp and bright
Winter is here with snow so white
Flakes fall like dancing lights
Why is winter such a wonderful sight

Icicles hanging like swords of steel
Rooftops glistening like diamonds so real
Ice on the ground
It is quiet all around

I'm snug and warm inside my bed
No sign of cold around my head
Jack Frost cannot bite me tonight
Because I'm tucked up nice and tight

With the season at an end
The trees are now beginning to mend
The spring is near where buds will appear
We will now have to wait another year.

Brett Evans (11)
Thomas Telford School, Telford

The Haunted House

In the furthest outskirts of Transylvania
A desolate house stands
Occasionaly racked by the wind
The house echoes with the constant wind howling
And doors creaking
For something terrible lies within the house
Worse than the end of the world

In the overgrowing forest
Many animals live
The neighbours fear the bloodthirsty
Vampire!
No human has ever seen him
And lived to tell the tale!

Rhys Wenlock (11)
Thomas Telford School, Telford

Distance

There's a cry in the distance,
My people gather round
Should we go or should we stay?
Then there was no sound!

All I saw was a man on his back
With his legs up in the air,
He looked rather paralysed
But I couldn't stop and stare!
Someone called for an ambulance
And they were quickly there!

He recovered slowly but well,
Will not yet go to Heaven or to Hell!
All he does is thank us now,
We have no need to forgive!
We knew everything would be alright
As long as he just lived!

Sophie Percox (12)
Thomas Telford School, Telford

The Disowned

I was like an old can of Coke and a stone in one,
disowned and left to rot
oblivious to anyone and everything
I sat on the cold, hard curb
I was the eyes of the world
feeling the neglect from the onlookers passing by.
They did not know how lucky they were
they just took all the flash cars
and big houses for granted,
not even thinking about the less fortunate people,
such as myself.
I wouldn't mind it so much
if it wasn't for the abuse.
Verbal mostly but sometimes even physical.
The spit in the face summed my life up,
rejection
and neglect.
Sometimes I even bother to beg,
not ask.
Beg.
Do you know how that feels?
The rejection I feel.
If only they could see the world
from my eyes
if only.
In their eyes
I would never be one of them.
As I as born one and am one.
A reject.

Liam Ward (11)
Thomas Telford School, Telford

I Wonder What It Would Be Like To Be An Athlete

I wonder what it would be like to be an athlete,
Getting up every morning to train,
Training till dark when the stars are out.
You get home dripping with sweat.

I wonder what it would be like to be an athlete,
The cheer of the crowd,
Screaming,
Nerves pumping round your body.
Go. With all your energy, you sprint to the end of the track.

I wonder what it would be like to be an athlete,
The crowd cheering you and other countries booing.
Circling the stadium with a massive smile on your face,
An England flag around your shoulders as you walk.
You step up to get your gold medal.
The crowd going crazy till they're dead on the floor.

I wonder what it would be like to be an athlete.

Alex Berridge (11)
Thomas Telford School, Telford

What Would It Be Like?

As soon as I wake up,
I must look in the mirror,
Quickly get changed,
Pretty in pink,
Long lashing legs
Of the hairbrush,
Move around my hair,
Trying to break free from the knots.

Tap,
As high heels walk
Along the cold marble floor,
Step into the bathroom,
I start applying make-up,
To my chalk-pale face,
Spray flowery perfume,
My lips are a lipgloss bottle;
Shiny and sweet.

It's nearly the end of the day,
I have blisters on my feet,
My hand aches from
Endless hair flicking,
My blond hair isn't as
Shiny as glass anymore,
What can I do?
I must be perfect.

I think to myself . . .
I'm so glad
That, that isn't me.

Hannah McGilvery (11)
Thomas Telford School, Telford

Through The Eyes Of An Old Guitar

I sit here,
Day after day,
For someone to take me down,
From my dusty shelf,
No one loves me anymore,

My strings are rusty,
My paint has peeled,
I'm completely out of tune,
My neck is scratched,
My body is marked,
No one seems to care anymore.

I'm torn and tattered,
Sad and glum,
I have new friends,
But not for long,
For soon they will be gone,
No one loves me anymore.

I'm just a tree without bark,
Once shiny and new,
Time has passed so quickly,
I'm just an old guitar,
No one loves me anymore.

Hannah Loffman (11)
Thomas Telford School, Telford

A Place To Belong

Rough skin, beautiful face,
ragged clothes, no shoes,
bruises seeping through
the old ragged jeans.
All alone,
a wandering soul.

A loving spirit,
waiting to be held,
it is unwanted,
rejected,
sitting alone,
the treacherous cold,
eating away at her body.

Trembling, shaking,
the ice-cold demons have entered
her angelic soul.
Lips blue, chilblains irritating
her fragile fingers
and dainty toes.

Thud! Her head hits the ground,
her eyes elegantly close,
her distressed frown fades
and her natural beauty reappears.
She glows like an angel,
full of life and soul,
she has now found a place to belong!

Kirsty Hampton (12)
Thomas Telford School, Telford

Autumn

Autumn has come around again
A special time of year
The autumn leaves fall off the trees
And the air is very clear.

The leaves are brown and crispy
Falling to the ground
They fall so silently
Not even making a sound.

The trees lay bare
And the nights draw in
As the sky gets dark
The shadows swift through the trees
Like ghosts against the bark.

The squirrels hunt for brown nuts
And the birds sing sweetly and clear
The squirrels know by collecting their nuts
That frosty nights are near.

Carla Bithell (11)
Thomas Telford School, Telford

On The Beach

I feel the pebbles hot and smooth beneath my feet,
Digging deeper with my toes they are cool,
Some as cold as ice.

The sea was green like grass, cool and inviting,
Waves edged with foam, crash gently on the shore,
I lie back to see the sun looking down on me,
High bright and hot in the sky,
I close my eyes to hear an almost musical sound,
Like fingers running along a piano.

Evie Hope (11)
Thomas Telford School, Telford

I Wonder Why

I wonder why birds can fly,
How they glide across the sky.
I wonder why humans talk
And why we humans learn and walk.

I wonder why frogs eat flies,
Are they tasty like cottage pies?
I wonder why fish swim
And their bodies are slimy and slim.

I wonder why rabbits hop
And how their ears are long and flop.
I wonder why bees eat honey,
Do they sell it for lots of money?

I wonder why this poem rhymes
And why I've read it so many times . . .
I wonder why.

Adam Billingsley (11)
Thomas Telford School, Telford

The Trees

The trees were swaying in the wind,
Grabbing me as I walked by.
I called out for help but no reply.
The mist and the wind went away,
The trees stopped moving, still
And from that day on
I saw the bright shining sun.
No mist, no wind,
Just peace.

Akala Campbell (11)
Thomas Telford School, Telford

Visiting The Pioneer Centre

Going to the Pioneer Centre was great,
The coach chugged along like a train
Or some kind of mechanism.
The hut was great but it was decorated
Like a Christmas tree with tinsel and stars.
The food we ate was terrible (yucky stuff).

Going to the Pioneer Centre was not so fun,
We slept in bunk beds, I slept near a window
My feet were really cold just like a pail of water
Or a sodden handkerchief. Very wet.

Going to the Pioneer Centre was a bad idea,
We climbed walls and towers
Sometimes my legs hurt but each bar pushed me
Up higher with every step I took.
Going to the Pioneer Centre was maybe not a good idea -
Or was it?

Annalisa Parrino (12)
Thomas Telford School, Telford

Alton Towers

I arrive at the park
Seeing the sights,
The people screaming
From all the frights.

Looking at the rides
Looking at the big ones,
Deciding which to go on
Deciding the ride with the metal of tonnes.

I step on the roller coaster
Shaking with fear,
The wind in my eyes
Brings out a tear.

Now it's time to leave
The day is done,
Time to go home
That was fun!

Tom Carnduff (12)
Thomas Telford School, Telford

My Last Day Of Buildwas

It's the day today,
We leave forever,
No way,
Forever and ever.

You'll always be a friend to me
And that's the way it should be.

I don't want to see our friendship end,
So we will stay in touch and you'll still be my friend.

We'll email and telephone,
You'll still be able to hear me moan.

You'll always have a fond place in my heart,
But now it's time to make a new start.

Chloe Jones (11)
Thomas Telford School, Telford

Christmas

Christmas Eve, just can't sleep
Having fun, need to peep
Rudolph is coming, better leave him a snack
I hope Santa comes with his sack!
Snowmen are smiling in the snow
Time for Santa to say hello.
'Merry Christmas!' my mum shouts
As I rip open the presents and I am out
Sledging down the hill, screaming, having fun
Finally Christmas has come.

Ryan Turner (11)
Thomas Telford School, Telford

The Ice Rink

The ice looked strong and sturdy
Wow I never knew it was this big
And so many people
I looked at the ice
It sent a shiver down my spine
It felt like the ice was speaking to me,
'Come on Em hop on and skate
Enjoy yourself a little.'

The ice looked strong like a brick wall
It was fun when I got onto the ice
I never knew how fun ice skating was
It felt cold like walking into a freezer
I wish I had put an extra pair of socks
And another jumper on
But what can you do?

It was the best feeling when I was skating
It was hard to stand up for 10 minutes
But it was fun anyway
I didn't want to leave it was that fun
But we were going to McDonald's
So I thought why not, yum-yum.

Emily Key (11)
Thomas Telford School, Telford

Alton Towers

I am in the car and I am very nervous
I am not going on the Log Flume or the Corkscrew
I hate drops and I am scared of heights
I am in the park and I am very frightened.

The Corkscrew towers overhead,
'Not this one,' I anxiously said.
'Scaredy-cat,' mocked my brother, making me mad,
'Oh go on then, it can't be that bad.'
After the ride had ended this ride was my favourite.

'We haven't gone on the Log Flume yet,'
'Oh no, I really don't want to get wet.'
'Come on Son, it will be over in a flash,
Just watch out for the great big splash.'
After the ride had ended this ride was my favourite.

'Time for one more, what shall it be?'
'The Spinball Whizzer is not for me
I do not like being carried up so high.'
I really hope that I do not cry
After the ride had ended this ride was my favourite.

It is now the end of the day
I have really enjoyed it too
I love drops and I love heights
And I can't wait to come back and do it all again!

Andrew Balzan (11)
Thomas Telford School, Telford

My First Day At School

Ding went the bell,
People were talking loudly as they walked to the door,
I started to walk to the door in my pristine uniform.
Everyone went inside and the playground was left,
Like a deserted desert.

Bang went the door as it shut.
The teacher stood like a mountain in front of my year,
She introduced us to the other teachers, who looked frightening,
By this time I wanted to go home.

The teachers took us to our classrooms,
The long corridor walls stared at me,
The whole school was a big maze trying to make me lose my way,
My heart was beating like a ticking clock.
How will I remember it all tomorrow!

James Cox (11)
Thomas Telford School, Telford

My Cat

He creeps through the alley,
Like a burglar nicking goods.
He's silent but deadly,
Like a bird waiting for prey.

He slaps and scratches the air,
As if it's playing with him.
He jumps through the air,
As high as a tree.

He snatches at the flying thing,
As if he's been well trained.
He pulls it down and tears it apart,
As if he's a military soldier.
He makes it cry and makes it scream,
Like a child who's lost its toy,
He's deadly
And he's my cat!

Henry Craven (11)
Thomas Telford School, Telford

When The Circus Isn't Fun Anymore

You can hear them crying out loud,
The tamer just looks at them and smiles.
He can see them in pain, but will not help.

They swing their trunks and start to yelp,
'Roll up, roll up,' the keeper chants.
The animals pray they won't today.

No one takes notice of their pleas,
They walk towards the big top,
The animals suffer for the tourists' greed.

Why won't they listen?
Why don't they care?
They say their life can be unfair!

Distressed, in pain -
Just more money to gain.
All for profit -

They took it one step too far -
Shackles round our legs - wires and chains
Around our necks,

This isn't right -
There is more to life than meets the eye.
Why can't they see it then?

The phrase,
'Dance puppets, dance!'
Springs to mind . . .

A life in showbiz -
What a joke!
They leave us here to sit and croak . . .

A life of misery - a life of pain
What a joke
And you thought circuses were fun!

Lexie Millington (11)
Thomas Telford School, Telford

The Flame

The flame is so beautiful,
It has power you and me are daring to believe,
It can cause tragedy,
It can cause devastation,
With complete power and ease.

Some people fear the flame,
Some people loathe it,
But you can't stand without marvelling at it,
The power,
The grace
And the warmth.

It has claimed many lives,
Killed innocent people,
The flame murders people,
The flame also saves lives,
It has the greatness to do both.

As the flame grows old it flickers and dies,
But it is always living, always breathing,
It has a life,
It is like a great spark of life,
Waiting to be snuffed out.

Ryan Sohier (11)
Thomas Telford School, Telford

The Wind

Howling wind screaming at me,
Trees creaking, leaves blowing,
Scattering under my feet,
The wind blowing like it's throwing itself at me.

Trees falling, crashing with a big bang,
Wind blowing strongly,
Making the waves bigger and bigger,
Wind chimes clanging,
Cars rolling away.

Laura Davies (11)
Thomas Telford School, Telford

If I Were In Your Shoes

Flying high in the sky above the trees and houses,
The wind whizzing past, such a nice cool breeze.
The view quite breathtaking,
I can see for miles and miles.

The people down below looking busy like ants,
Dashing this way and that way,
Rushing here and there.

I'm carefree and happy,
I can do whatever I like,
I can eat, sleep and play any time of the day.

I can fly to any country and sleep in any tree.
I can avoid the nasty weather and have worms for my tea.
I love being me,
I like what I do,
If you had a chance to be put in my shoes,
A bird is what you would be.

Oliver Leason (12)
Thomas Telford School, Telford

A Poem About A Storm

I looked through the window and suddenly the rain came.
I heard it banging on the roof above my head like machine-gun fire
And then came the thunder, booming loudly in the distance
And slowly creeping closer,
Until a deafening *clap* exploded above my head.
Next the lightning flash sent spears of light hurtling across the sky.
I heard the wind rushing around the house
Like a steam train leaving a station
Gathering speed
Rushing and swirling like the arms of a windmill
It was very alarming
Then just as suddenly the storm was gone,
Moving away to surprise another boy
In another town.

James Burton (11)
Thomas Telford School, Telford

Charlie's Morning

Sitting patiently in my box,
my tail waiting to wag,
footsteps,
Master, coming down the stairs,
doors unlock.

Paws damp with dew, squelch muddy borders,
sun glows a huge smile, greeting the new day,
sniffing scents around the garden, watching bees buzz by,
lights come on in neighbours' bedrooms,
Master's voice demanding a return back inside.

Cat munching and crunching on his food,
my name is called; Master feeds his faithful servant,
same food every day.
Master gets ready for work,
shoes so shiny, other dogs smile back.

Treats for good boys, safe in pockets,
walking companions, proud protector
friends in fields,
spotty, dotty Dalmatians race, graceful greyhounds.

Master out for hard day's work,
Charlie on bed all snug and warm.

Matthew Langman (11)
Thomas Telford School, Telford

A Wonderful Life

I once had a wonderful life,
Filled with running and jumping,
My soft cotton wool bed,
The sweet smell of my dinner.

My body strong and magnificent,
I always came first in any race.
My legs strong and powerful
How I wish those days were once more.

There is nothing familiar about this place,
The cold cobbled streets,
The bare brick walls,
Is this my new home?

My fur is wet,
I am tired and hungry,
Where is my home
Where I was once loved and cherished?
Not here!

The children are long gone
They loved to come and play,
I used to adore *fetch the ball,*
But now,
It is all a survival game.

The bright colours of life
That used to surround me,
Have all gone.
All I see now
Is the greyness around.
I once had a wonderful life.

Nitesh Patel (11)
Thomas Telford School, Telford

The Tsunami

I cry for help but nobody can see me,
I shout for help but nobody can hear me,
The wind is so strong, I can't hold on much longer,
Somebody help me!

My island is no longer, the water surrounds me.
Everything is destroyed,
Trees,
Cars,
Houses.
I feel so alone and frightened,
What should I do?
Somebody help me!

This place is like a floating graveyard,
Bodies everywhere.
Where are my family,
Are they down there?
Somebody please save me!

Ashley Robson (12)
Thomas Telford School, Telford

Unwanted Furball

Scared and frightened furball, lonely, unhappy,
Searching for food in the empty dustbins.
Afraid, hungry, cold and unwanted, uncared for!
Can hear barking, runs but is too weak!
People walk past but don't even speak!
Walking the streets, sniffing, sniffing.
Barks at the people, wanting help.
But no one speaks a word back.
Scratches, yelps, barks, but he seems invisible!
Suddenly he feels something on his back!
He sees a hand stroking his fur.
A wanted dog looks up to a kind, happy face.
The dog yelps and barks with joy!
A happy person takes him home!
She feeds him, plays with him!
The dog has found an owner!

Priya Moore (11)
Thomas Telford School, Telford

Living On The Streets

People stare in the street,
But I don't really mind,
Looking at my smelly, shabby clothes,
As though I've crossed the line,

My hair tangled like rats' tails,
My face an expressionless brick,
I've lived on the streets for many a year now,
It's made me really ill,

I have to steal to eat,
Just to keep me alive,
Whether it's just a rotten apple core,
I'm not bothered, it's food,

I wish someone would help me,
Give me a better life,
Or at least just give me a proper home,
But some people are as sour as old sweets,

They won't give me a chance,
They *didn't,*
Yes,
I'm not alive,
I caught a bad disease,
And that was all,
From living on the streets.

Rachel Price (11)
Thomas Telford School, Telford

I Wonder

In darkness, I live.
Also in curiosity.

I sit here and wonder,
What,
What would it be like to see
The wonders of the world?
To be as free as a bird,
To adore bright colours,
People and animals.

I feel neglected,
Yet loved.
Alone,
Yet crowded.

I sit here and wonder,
What,
What would it be like
To see the wonders of the world?

To travel and experience,
To watch a fire burning.
Shimmering red,
Blazing yellow and smouldering orange.
Just to see a single rose petal.

I sit here and wonder,
What,
What would it be like to see
The wonders of the world?

Sophie Smith (11)
Thomas Telford School, Telford

A Day In The Life Of A Fish

When the light pierced the surface
of the deep blue ocean
I saw the usual array of colour.

The coral that I saw
was as beautiful as ever,
this is my home.

Around the coral swam
a whole variety of fish.
They darted in and out of the coral,
the lights catching their skin
making them shimmer like sunlight on glass.

Mmm, what's that smell?
Bread!
Where is it, I must find it?
Look there it is
I'll have that for my tea.

Ouch! My mouth
there must have been a hook in that bread
Help! I'm being pulled towards the surface
I can't feel water, I can't breathe.

I must wriggle free, hey I'm falling
splash!

Jack Bennett (11)
Thomas Telford School, Telford

If Only I Could See

I am a blind female,
What would it be like,
If only I could see?

Would I be able to see
The greenness of an apple tree,
If only I could see.

What do clouds look like?
Do they really look so fluffy,
Like cotton wool?
If only I could see.

What about the sea,
All shimmery and blue,
All this I have been told
If only I could see.

I think about the sun,
Is it red, orange or yellow?
Is it big and round?
If only I could see.

Most of all I think about me,
I can't look in the mirror,
What would I see?
If only I could see.

Haley Barton (11)
Thomas Telford School, Telford

Homeless Cries

Sitting alone in the dark,
Late at night.
No dinner on my plate,
Just clear snowflakes
I can hear weeps from other alleys
How I wish I was with them.
Or anyone.

Can't get to sleep tonight,
Mom's working late.
Don't see cats' bright red eyes,
Strut past my so called 'home'.

I just wish people understand
What it's like to live a life like me.
To sit alone at the park in the day,
To lie in an alleyway most nights
Apart from 'my luxury' the shelter home,
On Tuesday, Thursday and Saturdays.

The shelter is my saviour,
That gives me the strength to wake up in the morning,
But if only they had more money,
All of us could live there 24/7.

Well maybe my dream will come true one day.
No more homeless cries.

Jeska Dimmack (11)
Thomas Telford School, Telford

Daisy Dog

I've wanted a puppy for ages
I've pestered my mum and dad
They've finally said I can have one
Oh boy, I'm really glad!

When we went to collect her
I was very clearly told,
'You're not to go wild around her
She's only six weeks old.'

When I finally met her
She came and sat on my lap
She looked so tired and scared
Then she snuggled up for a nice long nap.

We've had her now for five months
In the mornings she's really mad
She runs round the house
Then bolts up the stairs and jumps all over my dad!

Matthew Vernon (12)
Thomas Telford School, Telford

Braving The Beam

G etting ready to mount the beam, knees are knocking,
  heart is pumping but here goes . . .
Y es! I've landed my tuck back, nothing can stop me now
M y mind stays focused. I have to keep calm
N ow for the flick, let's keep it tight
A full spin next, an easy move . . . but many fall off
S plit leap to go, straight, stretched legs are essential
T his is it, time for the dismount . . . job done. Big smile.
  Crowd cheers.

Erin Arrowsmith (12)
Thomas Telford School, Telford

Winter

Winter slowly creeps,
His powers are awake
It destroys autumn and takes the world
Winter's plans become unfurled

It turns the wind ice-cold
And freezes the water still
It makes the animals tremble with fear.
It even scares the mighty deer.

Winter's clutch on the world is weakening
For there is another power awakening
Spring uses its flower power
And says it's winter's final hour.

Christopher Hodgetts (11)
Thomas Telford School, Telford

The Haunted House

There it stood
The haunted house in the wood,
It was dark and gloomy,
It really threw me.
Sticky cobwebs hung from the ceiling,
It gave me a creepy feeling,
The dark eerie house makes me feel so alone.
Oh how I wish I was safe at home.

The floorboards were creaking,
As I saw a monster peeping,
I climbed the stairs,
And on the back of my neck stood my hairs,
The dark eerie house makes me feel so alone.
Oh how I wish I was safe at home.

Jake Walters (11)
Thomas Telford School, Telford

Snow

S now, snow, tumbling down onto trees,
　　just like big candyfloss on sticks!
N umbing coldness on toes and fingertips
O utside you see razor-sharp icicles, hanging
　　down from the window ledges
W atermelon-sized snowballs toppling down on to you.

Hayley Aldridge (11)
Thomas Telford School, Telford

Holiday

When we go on our holidays,
We usually go to France.
My mum and dad like the food,
My sister likes to dance.

We take the ferry across the sea,
Then we travel by car.
It takes an age to get there,
Because it is so far.

I enjoyed swimming in the pool,
I also ride my bike,
All my friends are so cool,
And this I really like.

We sit and talk all evening,
Until it is quite late,
Sometimes when I stay out too long
My mum and dad are irate.

When the holiday is over,
And we return back home,
I am quite sad to leave France,
I always have a moan.

Jack Isgar (11)
Thomas Telford School, Telford

A Cold Winter Day

It's as cold as the Antarctic in the morning
No whistling birds to wake up to
Just the silence of miles of empty land.

The cold days in cold rooms,
The heaters are popular with everyone.
Everybody is dreading having to go back
Outside into the cold wide world.

The evenings are cold and the sky becomes dark early,
No time to stay out with your friends.
You have to come in before it gets dark,
You sit by the fire and hope for summer to come soon!

Hannah Perry (11)
Thomas Telford School, Telford

There Will Come Soft Rains

There will come soft rains
And the smell of the ground
The swallows circling
With their shimmering sound

Fish swim at night
And the sun blissfully bright
Children kindly play
All through the day

Then there's trouble
The children all flee
And the fish play
As the children did
Once before with glee.

George Wilkes (11)
Thomas Telford School, Telford

The Cup Final

I run and run and kick the ball,
Then someone kicks me and then I fall.
The ref blows his whistle and shouts, 'Oi!'
Then gives a yellow card to that other boy.

I take three steps back then three forward,
I strike the ball towards the goal,
Over the top of the wall,
It looks like it's going in -
Only the goalie to beat.
The goalie jumps and misses it,
'Yes!' What a goal from me.
I run towards the crowd as they cheer,
And celebrate (maybe later with a beer).
'Ten seconds left,' says the ref.
Then ten seconds later, the whistle blows.
What a win!

Daniel Quinn (11)
Thomas Telford School, Telford

Hallowe'en

The lights are dimmed
It's Hallowe'en
It's one of the times
My uncle shouldn't be seen.

He lives in a great dark house
So high on a hill
Even walking past
Gives you a *great big chill*.

He's the original Goth
Who only comes out at night
Just glancing at him
Will give you a fright.

He is excellent for Hallowe'en
The hint of his white teeth
Give away Count Dracula's secret
Which brings you a lot of grief!

Stacy Snook (11)
Thomas Telford School, Telford

This One's From Me

Basketballs and cricket bats,
But this one's from me.
Presents and cards,
But this one's from me.

Homework from teachers,
But this one's from me.
A letter from a friend,
But this one's from me.

Love and best wishes,
A personalised message,
Hugs and kisses,
This one's from me.

Natasha Hall (12)
Thomas Telford School, Telford

At Night

At night the wind rushes
howling like a bear
past my window and past my door
the wind whistles in the air.

At night the owls hoot loudly
in the wood nearby.
In the distance
I can hear the foxes cry.

At night the moon rises
getting bigger and bigger till it's whole
It lights up the sky
like a big silver bowl.

Sarah Robinson (11)
Thomas Telford School, Telford

My Mum

Her skin is as soft as the finest silk,
Her smile spreads warm, the golden kind,
Lilies the colour of the rainbow,
A brain as bright as Albert Einstein's,
Her long locks bounce through the air,
Laughter and bubble as pink champagne,
Hard -working is her middle name,
Sadly this is the end,
My mom, my friend.

Megan Holloway (11)
Thomas Telford School, Telford

My Grandad

I remember when I was small
Visiting you at Longnor
Sitting in the garden in the sun
Riding on your tractor, oh what fun.

Now you've moved to Codsall Town
And I know you've settled down
Even though your garden's quite small
You manage to enjoy it all.

You're such a great grandad and a friend to me
I have a fun-time when I come to tea
You show me your garden, laden with flowers
It's so beautiful as if made with special powers.

You've made a garden full of flowers
Where you can spend many hours
When it rains into your shed you go
Carving all the birds you know.

With your paints yellow, red and grey
In it you spend many a day
When nanny calls, 'It's time for tea.'
You walk up past the old yew tree,

It's market day when Wednesday comes
Where you go to meet your chums
The auctioneer shouts, 'Who will pay
To buy these ducks and geese today!'

Now it's one o'clock and so
Off to the Woodman pub you go
The dinner's great, so's the booze
No matter what food you choose.

Amber Richards (12)
Thomas Telford School, Telford

My Big Sister

My big sis is treated best,
But to me she's a pest!
It's not fair
She always stays up later than me!
The last time she got told off was in a different century,
She gets bigger portions of food
And she never gets told off for being rude!
All her clothes are better than mine
She's always looking cool and fine!
But . . .
Even though she's a little miss
She is my favourite big sis.

Charlee Skinner (11)
Thomas Telford School, Telford

Nocturnal Phobia

I'm scared of the dark
Like a pencil getting sharpened
Like a curly cucumber going *chip! Chop!*

I'm scared of the dark
Like a spider getting poisoned
Like a tile falling and going *smash! Bang!*

I'm scared of the dark
Like a black bat springing into the daylight
Like an aching Ankylosaurus getting eaten by T-rex.

I'm scared of the dark
Like bouncy bacon frying itself to smithereens
Like an egg going *crick! Crack!*

I'm scared of the dark
Like a volcano having gallons of water poured down it
Like a warrior getting hit in the last minute.

I'm scared of the dark
Like a tomato getting squished on the creepy chopping board
Like a buzzy bee going *zzzzzz! Bang!*

I'm scared of the dark!

Kiran Bhatia (11)
Thomas Telford School, Telford

The Light

Looking down on cuckoo green
One wet and dismal night
The green grass shimmered gently
Beneath the village lights

Beyond the wet village green
The lights reflected on the trees
Leaves on the branches shimmering
From the breeze across the green

The shadows on the houses
Across cuckoo village green
Broken only by the village lights
That shine around the green

In the sky high above the green
The lights look very small
Is the scene below a city
No, it's only cuckoo green.

Laura Guest (12)
Thomas Telford School, Telford

Winter

What do you think of when winter comes to mind?

I think of icicles glistening in the cold
And of course, the day that never gets old.

'Christmas!' We all cry,
While watching the sparkling stars in the sky.

The fantasy comes alive,
Like the reindeers on your drive!

But then all the magic fades away
At the very, very end of the day.

So that's what winter means to me,
But what is winter meant to be?

Hollie George (11)
Thomas Telford School, Telford

What Mum Said

'Head to the seaside,'
Mum said,
The day we went for a drive.

'You'll enjoy it . . . honest,'
Mum said,
The day we went for a drive.

'Look at the country!'
Mum said,
The day we went for a drive.

'First one to see the sea, shout rhubarb and custard,'
Mum said,
The day we went for a drive.

'We're going to sit on the sand with the waves lapping at our feet,'
Mum said,
The day we went for a drive.

'You'll be full up when you've eaten my gorgeous picnic under
the baking sun,' Mum said,
The day we went for a drive.

But Mum wasn't right!
I couldn't be bothered to look at the dreary countryside,
I wasn't the first to shout 'rhubarb and custard',
Have the sea lapping at our feet?
We couldn't even see the sea, it was that far out,
And as for sitting under the baking sun, eating lunch,
Well the heavens opened and it poured down.
The next morning at breakfast Mum said those dreaded words,
'Pack your bag Heather, we're going for a drive!'

Heather Jenkins (12)
Thomas Telford School, Telford

Goldfish!

Every day
You walk past my tank.
I race to the back behind the pirates' plank!
I know it sounds stupid,
But it's true -
I once was a human
With brains like you!
Though I am boring,
Though I am dumb.
Though when I use the toilet
I can't wipe my bum.
I know it sounds stupid,
But it's true -
I once was a human
With brains like you!
What shall I do today?
Shall I swim?
Will I die?
Life is grim.
I know it sounds stupid,
But it's true -
I once was a human
With brains like you!
So I'll splash around
Then flap my tail.
Larger than an ant,
Smaller than a whale!
I know it sounds stupid.
But it's true -
I once was a human
With brains like you!

Sophie Munger (11)
Thomas Telford School, Telford

The Killer Eagle

The eagle flies so elegantly through the air,
Her widespread wings can be seen for miles.
The beady eyes of this watching bird,
Searches for its feast among the valleys.
The eagle gazes at a vole sitting on a waterbed,
She swoops down and tears it to pieces.

The eagle's furry feathers ruffle as the wind passes by,
She senses something delicious.
The smell of rotting flesh draws her towards the ground,
A dead deer lies motionless by the riverbank.
It sits quietly and enjoys its tasty feast,
And then flies off, far into the distance.

Alex Grove (11)
Thomas Telford School, Telford

The Wolf

Silently it crept,
Silently its prey slept,
Silently it bared its teeth,
Silently it approached like a thief.

It stabbed its teeth into its prey's head,
It growled in joy as it was going to be fed,
It peeled of the flesh and picked at the skull,
It grabbed its prey and began to pull.

Slish, slosh went the mud as it passed,
Pit, pat went its feet as they hit the ground fast.
Rip, rip went the flesh of the prey's leg,
Squeal, squeal went its prey as it began to beg.

Silently it stopped and bared its teeth once more,
Silently the rain began to pour.
Silently it picked at its prey's chest,
Silently it thought, *this meal is the best!*

As it ate the meat of its prey, it thought,
I am happy to be a wolf.

Kieran Wallace (11)
Thomas Telford School, Telford

Killer Kitty

What a pretty little cat,
Sitting on Grandma's lap,
Purring softly while being stroked,
She takes her afternoon nap.

What a cunning little cat,
She creeps stealthily around the house.
She pauses and then pounces,
Her claws ripping apart the mouse.

What a friendly little cat,
My two sisters chase with glee.
They dangle wool in front of her,
And she paws it playfully.

What a lethal little cat,
Who's been lying on my bed.
Itching, sneezing and hardly breathing,
I fear I may soon be dead!

James Barker (12)
Thomas Telford School, Telford

Autumn

Autumn begins, golden leaves falling softly
Branches blowing in the wind, bare and brown.
Children playing with the leaves, crispy and crunchy
Acorns drop, conkers fall down.

Pumpkins are carved and beautifully lit,
Scary costumes, witches and screams,
Fireworks bright, round the bonfire we sit.
Toasting marshmallows, remembering what November 5th means.

Holly Mount (11)
Thomas Telford School, Telford

Rock Festival

Millions of long greasy-haired rockers went to Donnington Park,
Girls wearing skimpy clothes to get themselves noticed.
Boys in baggy jeans and leather cowboy hats.
They didn't want to be noticed.
Other than the boys who dyed themselves, red, green, yellow and blue,
Coloured from head to toe.
They got noticed!
They appeared in Kerrang magazine.

Everyone was there for the music,
Rock and alternative music,
Loud rock music.
Everyone has a good time because they leave deaf!
Enjoying the dangers of the mosh pit.
There were bands like Slayer, Slipknot, Feeder, Billy Idol -
These were the bands that I liked best.

Katie Taylor (17)
Two Rivers 6th Form, Tamworth

The Jeep Safari

On the leader jeep, driving through the hills;
Stopping to admire the view.
See the mountains and the hotels.

Revving in the dirt
Throwing dust behind
Creating a dust cloud.
Hot, tired, thirsty,
Wanting a rest.

Water pouring from a pipe
We drove under it and got wet.
Cooled, refreshed, wet!

We stopped off for dinner
Rice, chicken, salad
And left feeling full and renewed.

Then we drove to Turtles beach
But saw no turtles,
Only sand.
So it wasn't very interesting.

Cara Hatchett (17)
Two Rivers 6th Form, Tamworth

Good Times - Great Memories

I went camping with my dad
All the equipment piled up in Dad's friend's car . . .
His tent, my tent.
His bags, my bags
And away we drove.

Dad and me, together on the bike.
Motoring along the roads,
Setting off on a long journey . . .
Our holiday . . .
Going to a music festival.

The bike goes really fast,
It's really loud and really smelly
But I don't care cos I'm safe with my dad.
Together on the bike,
Setting out on an adventure.

Claire Griffiths (16)
Two Rivers 6th Form, Tamworth

West Ham Football Team Gets Promotion To The Premiership

28th May 2005 was a very important date.
Cardiff was a very important place.
We played Preston and *we won!*
We won the championship trophy
We won promotion to Premiership.

I was so happy,
My team was back in the Premiership.
I would rather my team was in the Premiership
Than the Championship.
And I was there, at the Cardiff Millennium Stadium.

To celebrate, we had champagne,
We won money,
We danced.
I caught a football shirt thrown from the bus
By Teddy Sheringham.

I was in London when the tour bus drove around London
And back up to Upton Park.
That's where I caught my football shirt.
Now we had to wait,
Wait for the first Premiership game of the season.

Aarron Cormill (16)
Two Rivers 6th Form, Tamworth

Buster The Dog

I've had him since he was a puppy
A little bundle of white fur with spots on.
He was bought as the family pet,
He played, he bit, he chewed.
He has chewed slippers, shoes, anything on the floor
A one-dog destruction chewer!
We go for walks.
Buster - my friend.

David Bott (17)
Two Rivers 6th Form, Tamworth

Sitting On Santa's Lap

As a young child I used to cry at Santa -
At the scary man with the white beard,
Asking to be taken off Santa's lap
But Santa kept bouncing me up and down on his knee -
Making me feel sick.
My parents kept smiling and nodding at me,
Dad saying, 'Don't be so scared.'
Encouraging me to sit with Santa,
Then, the flash of the camera
And it was over for another year.
I could escape.

When I was older I loved Santa,
I looked forward to sitting on Santa's knee
And getting a toy for being a good girl.
They still nodded and smiled
There was still the flash of a camera,
But now I was sad to get off his knee.
It was over for another year,
Finished!

Tanya Curtin (17)
Two Rivers 6th Form, Tamworth

My Dinosaur

When I was two I had a heart operation,
I remember sitting up in my hospital bed
Watching the Lion King before I went for my operation.

Mum was scared - she used to cry a lot,
My dad was pretty scared but he didn't want to show it.
I wasn't scared. I was too young. I didn't understand.

My mum bought me a dinosaur when I was little,
He's done everything with me.
An ugly dinosaur thing.

He went everywhere with me,
Even if I was going for a check-up,
It was just there.

I came out of the operation, everything was all blurry.
Including my dinosaur.
It was just there. We'd made it!

My dinosaur gave me strength,
He brought me luck.
I loved seeing it.

But one day I came home and found it in the bin.
His neck broken,
I cried for ages.

Beverley Sheldon (16)
Two Rivers 6th Form, Tamworth

My First Day At School

I was shy and didn't want to go to school,
I didn't know anyone.

And I didn't like my red top and black skirt.

I was scared to walk into my class,
In Mrs Ashley's class.

Someone sat by me,
I didn't know her name.
She was as scared as me but we smiled at each other.
She helped me and I helped her.
By break time I was playing with this new girl,
A girl called Shauna.

Two weeks later we walked to school together every day.

Hannah Stokes (17)
Two Rivers 6th Form, Tamworth

Hear My Voice

Do not put me in prison,
It's not fair.
It's not right,
You must listen to my voice,
What I say is true.

I speak out
And I'm arrested.
In prison
In silence
Alone.

Here no one can hear my voice,
But they must not win.
I have to speak up
Speak out
Speak the truth.

I will talk to the walls of my prison
To the bricks
The stones will listen
The building will hear
Hear my voice.

James Grice (16)
Two Rivers 6th Form, Tamworth

Sort Out Your Mess God

Hey God!
You're too far up in the sky,
Get down here and listen to me.
This world that You made is a mess.

There are wars and fighting,
Man killing man.
Man killing animals,
Man killing God.

Get down here and sort it out,
This is Your mess.
You are the one who made the world,
You need to sort it out.

The world should be clean,
All the people should be good
Friends with each other
Helping each other.

But we need Your help
God helping people,
Helping us to sort out the world,
To sort out the mess.

Liam Farnsworth (17)
Two Rivers 6th Form, Tamworth

Father And Son

When I was little
Dad bounced me on his knee
The world went up and down
And I got dizzy.
But I was with Dad
He laughed at me and I laughed at him.
It was a special time
Father and Son
Alone, together,
In a world of bouncing and laughter.

Now we are grown up
There is no more bouncing.
No world of just father and son.
We still laugh
Occasionally,
But not that 'throw back your head,
Bouncing on knee,
World going up and down
Dizzying,
Carefree laugh.'

Andrew Forest (16)
Two Rivers 6th Form, Tamworth

Listening To Music

Listening to music

On the stereo
On the television
On the kareoke

In my bedroom
In the lounge
In the kitchen

Asleep
Awake
In my dreams

The music takes me to different countries
To the top of mountains
To the deepest sea

I feel happy
Excited
Peaceful

Listening to music -
Good times
Great memories.

Rebecca Partridge (16)
Two Rivers 6th Form, Tamworth

Young Writers Information

We hope you have enjoyed reading this book - and that you will continue to enjoy it in the coming years.

If you like reading and writing poetry drop us a line, or give us a call, and we'll send you a free information pack.

Alternatively if you would like to order further copies of this book or any of our other titles, then please give us a call or log onto our website at www.youngwriters.co.uk

**Young Writers Information
Remus House
Coltsfoot Drive
Peterborough
PE2 9JX**

(01733) 890066